11/6/20

Dear Jim,

Thanks for your patience in waiting for this book to arrive. Enjoy!,

Love,
Ell

Waitress at the Red Moon Pizzeria

Eleanor Levine

2016 Unsolicited Press Trade Paperback Edition
Copyright © 2016 Eleanor Levine
Preface by Jaime Manrique
Photographs by Brian Healey
All characters, events, etc., are fictional; any coincidence is purely illogical.
Editors: Nicole Pomeroy and S.R. Stewart
All Rights Reserved.
Published in the United States by Unsolicited Press.

ISBN:0692636951
ISBN-13:9780692636954

For Bill Sullivan and Brian Brunius

Acknowledgments

David Ignatow, RHW Dillard, Katha Pollitt, Jeanne Larsen, Cathryn Hankla, Eric Trethewey, Jaime Manrique, Eileen Myles, Wayne Johnston, Clinton and Blanche Corbett, Trisha Conheeney, Michelle DeWitt, Julie Leonard, Eva Szybalski, Nancy Beckman, Jayne Wilkes, Brian McCarthy, Eugene Grygo, Jennifer Wasmer, Michele Oshima, Maria Herrera, the Gritzans, Beth Broome, The Sweets, Randi Levinas, Liz Kaplan, Bobby Ward, Emily Gordon, Robb Quattro, Lori Joseph, Kim Rhodes, Beth Monica, Kim Perez, Susan Hostetler, Rob Zseleczky, Lisa Amaker, Kelly Carlin, Bruno Lartiges, Brian Sanders, Khaki Rodway, Paul Pavese, James Kaston, Reynolds Tenazas-Norman, Pedro Silva, Frank Dietrick, Tom Raul, Howard Hecht, Mindy Shelkowsky-Pitonyak, Sharon Peterson, Michail Reid, Phillip Maltin, Sherry Aly, Tom Holland, Tony Romano, Audrey Szepinski, Michele Ingram, Tim Pyne, Melanie Huber, Lizzie Parks, Donna Epler, Lisa Bower, Mei Lei Inouye, Kyle and Tiffany Deacon, Kelley Shinn, Cort Bledsoe, Brandon Patterson, , the Billecs, the Andersens, the Schachters, the Zwisohns, the Hogans, and the Levines: Jack, Hilda, Allan, Stephen, Yvonne, Michael, and Jess.

Table of Contents

Preface

In an absurdist and surreal poetic world in which verbs have dandruff, and mothers go to "Wagnerian acupuncture lessons," anything can happen—and does. I applaud the glory of this extravagantly surprising, and touching poet. Eleanor Levine's voice is an invitation to smash all the clichés and to liberate the imagination from all the chains that civilization has created to enslave us. If Emily Dickinson had been a lesbian Jew from Brooklyn she could have written these riotous poems. After you read Levine, the world, poetry, life itself, seem newly minted.

—Jaime Manrique

Jaime Manrique is an award-winning author of the memoir *Eminent Maricones*, and the novels *Latin Moon in Manhattan*, *Twilight at the Equator*, *Colombian Gold*, and most recently, the critically acclaimed *Cervantes Street*. A contributor to Salon.com, *BOMB*, and other publications, he lives in New York City and is Distinguished Lecturer in the Division of Humanities and the Arts at the City University of New York (CUNY).

"Almost everyone wants to be the lover. And the curt truth is that, in a deep secret way, the state of being beloved is intolerable to many. The beloved fears and hates the lover, and with the best of reasons. For the lover is forever trying to strip bare his beloved. The lover craves any possible relation with the beloved, even if this experience can cause him only pain."

--Carson McCullers, *The Ballad of the Sad Café and Other Stories*

Artificial Limbs

for "Sweetie" [1]

Artificial limbs
are more than the synthetic joints and toes
sightable apparitions that permit
the live skeleton to indulge in his existence
it is the infrared eyesight
the eschewed reality
of a Danish psychiatrist believing there is
sunlight in Winter
or a born-again Southerner acknowledging that God
is a bathroom seat
or a dog believing that a tissue is food
or a man thinking his mistress walks glibly
down the shopping aisle
that Allen Ginsberg was a misogynist
because he had several affairs with women
or that Kurt Cobain died for our sins
or that red polish will hide your dirty nails
or that mice droppings can kill people
and artificial limbs dangle from New Zealand trees
where a daughter cries for love from your heart
and another wraps those limbs from
the pavement because she's afraid
or your friend, when he tells you,
he can get it up for 20 minutes
or the sister who needs a psychiatrist
tells everyone else they need one
or that Michael Jackson was really a woman
taking piano lessons
artificial limbs are our girlfriends who never kiss us
the homeless man who smells of urine and wants to be our friend
the dead fish, which, when thrown back into the water,

---

[1] The movie *Sweetie* (1989), directed by Jane Campion.

doesn't come to life
and the snarled reflections of a dead prostitute
who thinks he's literary
the quaky sound of an old British queen who wittily tells you
"crossword puzzles are the aerobics of the soul"[2]
or that Henry Miller has a stop sign between clauses
and Norman Mailer was a literary genius
and Susan Sontag's language is more visual than Leni Riefenstahl
and that amusing intellectual conversation
will redeem a thousand wounds
that by placing limbs in the arms of someone
or painting their house
you have given them a heart
it dies when you leave them up a tree.

---

[2] Quote from Quentin Crisp.

Two Friends

I gave Philip Levine a poem about prunes
Joseph Brodsky flirted with me
I've eaten rice and flounder at the Lamonts
Rockefeller took me to Ben & Jerry's for vanilla fudge
Charles Wright thinks my humor is ambidextrous
Rita Dove says mine is very intelligent
I get multiple orgasms in the cemetery
I have them at the Exxon Station
I date a blind Harvard lawyer
Mine's from Princeton—wears a wooden leg
My dad had tea with Eleanor Roosevelt
We own Helen Keller's umbrella
I lost thirty pounds after my cyst was removed
I was bulimic for six years and weighed less than Karen Carpenter
Reading Four Quartets *is like taking a shower with
God*
Wallace Stevens is LSD at the opera
I read poetry on Plaza Hotel bar stools
I was Norman Mailer's secretary
A janitor molested me at the YMCA
My aunt stuck her hand in my underpants
I type papers on kaolinite suspension for Colloids and
Interfaces
I edit testicular theories for Elsevier
My mother's cold
Mine is dead
I love you, Agnes
I'll love you when I feel like it

my dead roommate

my dead roommate
is not dead
but he looks
like an Auschwitz
victim
with his head
partly shaved
he thinks that
I'm a lesbian
and hate men
wish to drain
their testicles
down the bathroom sink
but I am
not a witch
nor am
I dead
I only wish
that he would
crawl away
and leave me
with slivers
of Sharon
Stone's blonde hair
upon my belly button.

Train

I.

Inside the apple seeds of a man's breath, with wooly facial hair—a migraine forest filled with the Unabomber's brain. I will not give him a blowjob through the Fruit of the Loom fibrous underpants where penis meets cotton. I smell the concerto of apple perfumes through lips and curling hair that lingers down his mouth—hairlines, an insignia forest—curling and looping brown/red threads upon his lips, hanging loose like below.

II.

A woman reads op-ed articles from the Columbia J School. Black and white opinion pieces with resilience because the course cost a thousand bucks in the spring; you leap through consonants and predicates and muffled phrases that have residual effects on your brain; she is inspired, with her leather boots and no-name nail polish, to exude intrigue with these papers, which she considers "commercially viable pieces."

III.

A priest opens to *Ephesians* in a leather-bound Bible with indented words; the pages are mangled and smell like tobacco. His dirty fingernails move with riveting speed, and as the Lord's servant, he says, "I love you, dear Jesus, you are my martyr and I am your humble crusader." The black lady on his left smiles, and continues reading *The Crucible*.

Thysanura

Gray nymphs
crawl on the ceiling
Mother says it is dust,
my dust, that makes
the silverfish
dance rapidly
propeller toes
in corners
where you can't
quell them unless
they pose naked under
a light and
we squash
the insides
with a grin

Minnie

moist as baked salmon
a verse from
William Carlos Williams' last meal
my Mother knew Minnie
and her husband Moe
with ruby whiskers
who lived in a brick building
near Red Moon Pizzeria
and Lane Drugs
"Minnie Mouse has rubber lips,"
I said when Mom made me visit
we brought diabetic chocolates
& a quart of milk
to her apartment,
which smelled
like gray hairs in the medicine cabinet
we sat in the dark since
Minnie didn't use a lamp
she and Mom spoke
about matzo
eggs and
the items on sale
at Shop Rite
that week

when Minnie died
we no longer
went to her place
near Jamesway
where Welfare recipients
made glamorous purchases.

Daddy and the Cicadas

When Daddy was dying
he watched the Mets
"Been there, done that," he said
like the kids in school

Now he eats cicadas
like a wild bandit
when they crawl on the ground
every 17 years

Daddy likes Archie and Edith
though Edith died at 90
sitting in front of the TV
with him and Mommy

They were discussing politics
Humphrey was nominated
the police beat Jerry Rubin
with a baton in 1968

I worry about Daddy
stuck in the ground
with no Worcestershire sauce
to put in his tomato juice

"Daddy and Mommy,"
we'd say at home
back from college
or a trip to New York

When Daddy died,
he met the cicadas
watching the Mets
after 17 years.

Pipic[3] Truths

Today I revised a
a rambling chapter
by Dr. Pypec
for his diabetes book.

*

Mother screamed,
*"Shut up—and the
good child gets
the soup's pipic!"*

*

My boss was baffled
that Mother fed us
boiled belly buttons
from chickens.

"Imagine her
chasing roosters
with a Walmart scalpel,"
I laughed.

"No, hens hatch,
don't have buttons;
you cook a cow's *outie,*
tender and spongy hot."

*

---

[3] Yiddish for navel or belly button.

In *Operation Shylock*,
Roth's main character,
Moishe Pipik,
is an imposter.

*

In the Old Testament,
Song of Solomon,
"Thy navel is like a round goblet,
 which wanteth not liquor."

*

The Chinese refer
to it as "shénquè,"
and Russian mommas put
deer lichen on for easy births

*

My umbilical dip is
anointed with fragrant oils,
though I never wore a bikini
after chicken soup.

The Follower

He was her Jesus Christ
and she was his apostle

Together they sang about
fecal matters and other elements

in the backyard where she
ate or killed squirrels

or rabbits that trampled on
the wrong side of the tree

Whenever Jesus left for work,
the disciple would whine for

hours at the window in the living
room and await the cream cheese

and bagel that Hilda (his mother)
offered as communal fodder for

her poor digestive system marred
by pancreatic difficulties that even

Jesus couldn't cure, although they
tried numerous remedies that cost

about twelve grand, where Eastern met
Western medicine in the vet's office

Finally, she stopped breathing
and biting and he
  could no longer find the teeth marks
she always left on his hands

Mammalah[4]

for Donna Tartt

the day Mammalah
died for
our sins
hyacinths
dripped
with mud

angelic
bluebirds
flew in flocks
and
yelped
in muted ecstasy

a moon
passed
over the sun
an eclipse
in the face
of a Swedish Hound

dogs came with laptops
poodles were selling
melted ice cream
Dobermans were
howling
in Yiddish

a mile
of
bitches and spouses
waited for

---

[4] "Mother" in Yiddish.

irretrievable
dog bones to
drop from the sky

the world
began with
a bark
and ended with a bark.

Mămăligă[5]

I eat almonds meant for baking.
My brother is not amused.

At Auschwitz they wouldn't be particular.
Zyklon B made *it* acceptable—sewing
Warsaw Ghetto rats in omelets.

*

Mother mixes peanut butter and apples,
lemon in coffee.
mămăligă with sour cream and cottage cheese.

She recalls French-Canadian slurs in hail;
mămăligă kept her full.

Our stomachs have changed,
but we are still Yids.

---

[5] Romanian peasant food cooked by boiling water, salt and cornmeal.

At Delicious Orchards[6]

humming since the Pharaoh
first stored colonies
in a desert apiary
black-eyed peas dancing
on hexagonal wax vestiges
hung from bellybuttons
off their momma
zizzzzzzg
spinning headlong
into each other and their
vast nest of Christ-like
followers who merge
year round
even when snow
covered our feet
and we knew
it'd mean ripples
of flesh
bitten by
brown/yellow tenants
if you threw
a rock into their
condominium

---

[6] At Delicious Orchards in Colts Neck, New Jersey, in the 1970s, they displayed a glass beehive case with hundreds of honey bees.

Daddy

he was a thin man
with lips tighter than Nebraska dirt
and bristles on his chin
I wanted to touch his face
but instead felt the stomach
and kissed him there
and asked, "Why are you
taking my Daddy?"
The people politely didn't
know what to say, but
wrapped him in a big
sack. The man who spoke
about goiter and
read the *NY Times* on Sunday
morning and called the dog "Rocko"
was assigned to a funeral
home. A few moments before
I played solitaire with his fingers and
he danced in front of me. The quiet
moments are upon us. I'll never
tell him how much I loved his
short stories. Each word and phrase
like a fingernail.

Barnegat

Bloated fish from the sea
on the concrete pavement
against the sandy stone

Below an ocean of green thread
a hook stuck in kelp

When I twist my rod
it gets caught

At three alone by the sea
I took the fish and threw it in the water
It was supposed to come back

They'd be tuggin' at our lines
catfish with Walt Whitman whiskers
black shiny flesh
bones floppin' in the air

We sit in our cars
while others eat subs

We never catch fish
only the weather on the radio

Before houses went up
flounder came reelin'

By the railroad tracks
the smell of seaweed
where my feet get splinters

You see crabs, lots of red meat, never ours

Afterward, Daddy takes us for soup
and we eat fish in the diner

Poem About Prunes

prunes
are soft
cockroaches
dripping with water

my father
cooks prunes
with raisins and
lemons
and boils
them
they help him
with his bowels

Grandma
is a prune
because she
is a Puerto Rican Jew
who dyes her hair yellow

King David eats
boiled prunes
on a silver plate
in a Jerusalem castle

Haman
inspires
sweet ironies
from a bakery

Alice B. Toklas
cooks prunes
for Gertrude Stein
baked with
juices and *juices*
and *juices*

Paul Fussell
sleeps in a brown wrinkled bed
at the Trench Hotel
"I am lying in
my large prune—
this is the cold
mother I never loved"

Stephen King
eats prunes
while screening
his imagination
(this makes
academics jealous
because he is on
the best seller list and
they are not)
"flying round soft
succulent swamps with
crawling raisins killing
fish through their digestive system…"

Jodie Foster absorbs
new obsessions
eating prunes
from a box
"Cardboard serenity," she says
"This is like a *really human*

thing to do even though I make seven million a year"

envoi

Prunes turn intellectuals
into human beings
and parents into
loving diarrhetics

Ida

for Gertrude Stein

Ida is my dead grandmother
She told me to wash the floor
I vowed I would always
needn't worry with her
fluffy hair
Ida died the night
of my forensics tournament
spoke from the Heavens:
"Don't forget Mr. Clean"

When I graduated from college
I became a maid at the Hyatt
walked in on two Germans
making love and returned
with ammonia
So when *Deutsche über alles*
had finished they would
not hear a pragmatic
Yiddish lady screaming.

Jack: A Dialogue

Mom, can you write a poem about
Daddy over the phone?
He was...
You got me at the wrong time...
My mind isn't functioning...
She laughs
Why do you want a poem about your father?
Iambic pentameter?
You need it to rhyme?
At six feet tall
and very spare
he wasn't fat (I'm telling you
what the word spare means)
a wonderful sense of humor
a friend
a lover
Was he good in bed?
A lover answers everything
All mine

E's Baseball

Lincoln Tunnel car fumes,
hot chestnuts in wax paper,
Hershey bars with orange peels,
screaming "Hank Aaron!"
"Babe Ruth!" as brother
hides in Shea Stadium.

He bought nose-bleed seats
near God, and fumed with
swirling swastika eyes as I
viewed *Goebbels Diaries,*
not Tom Seaver's strikeout
of the Chicago Cubs.

We won forty dollar Mets tickets,
saw the pizzaz of cleats,
butts hanging loose in field—
legs striding toward dugout,
Darryl Strawberry snorting
the great white dust.

At the Phillies' game:
four dollar hot dogs and indigestion,
Jersey girls/boys shrieking,
heros in dust, which precluded
me skimming Nazis, though I
cheered mightily for Michael Vick.

First Girlfriend

instead of Rilke,
she hums the Garden State Parkway Blues
reads a Pisces horoscope
plays guitar at the nursing home
and meets her husband

her mother,
who makes cheesecake,
has Alzheimer's

her Orthodox Jewish sister
has grandchildren and
her uncle says I'm a dyke
while driving me home

those who love her are
Miramax executives
the Mayor of Philadelphia
musicians, pediatricians,
taking photos
of violets, hoping their
daughters will be violets
boys who didn't come out
while Daddy was in prison
they snap pictures
or visit Paris in spring

everyone has a skeleton
in the closet,
hers are a pair of JCPenney jeans

Insecurities in a Sentence

I like my insecurities
they float around me
like goldfish crooning
or poets snapping like piranhas
in a Dewey Decimal System of juxtaposition
metaphors strung out on anxieties
claustrophobic participial phrases
verbs with dandruff
the wildness of a presumed innocence
of my Grandma grasping for ideas
the quiet interruptions of a stupid person
like overt silence in an African opera
light bulbs turned on in twilight
God plucking his chin hairs
Paul Fussell nourishing his ego
AA meetings where people sip coffee
and drift into thoughts about their neighbors
italicized bananas that look like Crayola crayons
rubbers that have holes in them
insecurity in a sentence
without a spinal tap of reality,
or a scissor tap dancing toward metaphors
the flux and influx in a flood in a bathtub
like a string in a tampon
or the boy on the platform with the muted sensibility
the playwright disdaining his ideas
or a cockroach taking ambidextrous steps toward his food
Allen Ginsberg snapping photos from his verses
Walt Whitman dancing naked on a tree stump
a stroke of light fanning its way to me at an opera
Bruce Springsteen chasing girls in the back seat of his car
Ezra Pound making scientific indentations in his poetry
I like the African of Afrikaner insecurity
and the bellhop kissing the bellhopper

I like the freedom that comes
from losing your soul to a pair of boys on the F train at 2 a.m.
the stuttering of Betty Friedan's motherhood
or the face of Kate Millett
who beams at the torn leather of her girlfriend's new boots
taut strings bend me in a sentence

ενέργεια[7]

muscles cut from
Michelangelo's David
and Plato's retreat
in a symposium
of Greek boys
and Oxford dons
who keep women
in an attic
at Rochester's house
while frail ladies
move in shadows
to the lighthouse
Madame Bovary
inhales
arsenic
Frida Kahlo
bakes for
Leon Trotsky
Marilyn kisses
Dan with
good teeth
in the
Rose Garden
near Senators
who sit in
all-white golf clubs
shooting balls
through holes

boys in junior high

[7] Means "Energia" or "energy" in Greek.

read myths
Icarus' wings melt
he falls.

Pallidotomy

*A destructive operation on the globus pallidus,
done to relieve involuntary movements or
muscular rigidity.* —Stedman's Dictionary

she assuages madness
by cultivating
lyricism on the page

a double dose of
aphrodisiacs and she
wanders in her robe
eating cereal
watching TV

thereafter
blood sweeps
like an ocean

remnants of an old
lady fill the room
benign thoughts
like popcorn.

Conduit

I had an MRI
where death tapped
on my postern in the
silhouette of a dorsal tumor

I prayed:
prevent entrance
to the white
tunnel

We will meet later
for tea, I advised him.

Lunch Drawing

for Adrian Holmes

A Greek penumbra spills itself
on a page in pencil and

a Georgian court with columns
is reflected through the shadows

the stoicism of it all, the finger indentation
the architect's work becomes art

with a spindle of thread called lead.

High School

the loudspeaker featured melancholy voices
(except when the valedictorian shrieked—
that was the only time the drug dealers
and steroid-induced football players petitioned that
Adam Sandler recite the Pledge of Allegiance)

a teacher who drew fluids from dead cats
found Rice Krispies while dissecting them
this was not the prestigious physics course
where dry minds studied mechanics and light

one boy smelled like Newark
made passes at students who forced his neck
through the film projector booth

Genghis Khan taught algebra
believed that x-y was holier
than the birth of Christ
discussed politics between equations
preferred Ford to Carter
you could never argue D wasn't
your destiny between fractions

a "friend" put a rubber on the lunch table
I picked it up while the entire cafeteria howled
in unmitigated hysterics

during Chemistry class
a jock put sulfuric acid down the Levis
of a 300-pound man-boy
with craters deep enough for astronauts

in the library
lesbian nuns studied Thomas Aquinas
while pimpled ex-seniors flirted with cheerleaders
because they had not done so in the 1950s

I got a C in sewing class
put the needle through my finger
might have stuck it through tits
if they had played Rachmaninoff

a boy hissed during readings of the *Iliad*
I wept the death of poets
who could not compete with Howard Stern

ghosts who travel along the lake used to ride cars
now walk through the dermatologist's office
with little boys who resemble them

Amor non reciprocatus

my bearded scholar
would I be less the woman
if I raped you tonight?

a horse gallivanting in the winds
you are gnawing my fields

snow flies above the sand dunes
piercing your mind
on an empty horse

the earth
shatters at
the tinkle of
bells

bouncing in a field of
flowers
I am lowering
you to the end
of Christendom

coming at you
like horses fleeing their
white masters.

Cinéma vérité

last night I saw
a clitoris
cut out of a female
the midwife stabbed
the girl's parts
and she died

afterwards
a movie
about Tibet
and one on South Africa
and the seventy-year-old editor
of the *Jerusalem Post*
slid his hand on
my thigh while
Tibetans were being murdered
I let him keep it there
because I wanted to travel to
Israel and get a byline

Like the time Quinn took his
tongue and thrust it in me
when I was five years old
or the African midwife
who took a piece of
flesh in the name
of Somali culture and virginity
and while Buddhist nuns were
butchered, the editor of the
Jerusalem Post moved
against me, like the girl without
the clitoris
moving against me

or when I call women

speak hostile on the phone,
wring my name in their ears
for I am the victim and the victimizer,
the clit and the clitorizer,
and I apologize to the girl at Film Forum
for stalking her

my brother Harry tells me that even
the editor of the *New York Times* shouldn't
touch you during the movies.

Herod's Gate

Brown eyes follow in the mid-morning
                    universe
of our Lord Jesus, who sings
between pews

I take the cross and
put it to my face where

God
walks through Arab ladies
between stone walls

there are oranges
and many plums

an Arab woman lies at her
feet hating mine

just yesterday
a mailman
who grew near the
tree
told me about
the olive
and how its
birth meant
another tree
betwixt stone walls
that our Lord Jesus
built while the temples
fell on the ground
where the Arab ladies
hate me.

The Electric Menorah

Bobby Meyer's crucifix lit the block:
a white/orange eclipse that kept
thieves from stealing baseball cards.

*

Ours was the bulkiest menorah in Jersey,
fluorescent lights among Mother's plants.

*

We kept up with the Cohens
their emaciated Hanukah bush—glittering
gold ribbons weighing more than branches.

*

A family of Hasidic Jews moved
and were startled by the effulgence
that ridiculed Sabbath.

*

Children threw candy at our door
soaped the car windows;
The New York Times was muddy.

*

We quit playing kickball and went to Rutgers;
big-bellied ladies with kids traversed the neighborhood.

*

While sitting *shiva,*
they brought herring and challah.

*

Mother keeps up with Hellenism,
setting the menorah in the window,
but only a few bulbs flicker.

Thirteen Faces of My Violin

For Wallace Stevens

perimeters of a woman's body

•

inside a holy
tomb for Egyptians

•

a case
with purple fur
the coffin

•

the bow
a sail mast for Lilliputians

•

little children play kickball
I butcher Boccherini

•

my posture bends
with the wooden lamb

•

Mother drives to
Wagnerian acupuncture lessons

•

polished wood
the skin

•

horsehairs
fill the room

•

a breadbox
playing music

•

a violinist sneers
while I fake

•

pages of a poetry book
smell like rosin

•

it lies under dust
in a broken case

Mima Hinda

I wept before her,
thinking it'd never happen,
but it did
sort of like this
or that
and then I thought, well, maybe
it won't, but it did,
just kept happening,
and before you turned,
she was gone,
no more Mommy
no more Mima Hinda,
just a wooden box
that held her.

*

Thirteen years earlier,
they put Daddy in a timber casket,
an American flag on top of
him, whom we called "Flathead."

*

After dirt hit Flathead's coffin,
she knew there was no Heaven,
but beckoned the rabbi to tell us there was;
we left them alone in the living room,
so she could have her moment with God.

Alligator

Like the raspy voice of a tooth surgeon
undermining the crops of India
you beleaguered us with your arrogance
Laughed when her pancreas exploded
Laughed as she lit the Shabbat candles
Laughed at her family—"those loose cables in a Florida theme park"
Drained us with a Roman cross
Met Joyce in Purgatory and burned his book
Stammered as if you were Jesus Christ
hanging laundry in the Bronx
And with tepid smoke breath
you spoon fed our brother's thoughts

Concertos in the Living Room

me, classical music,
listening to Mozart,
you, painting concertos

*

a violin gushes through
your/their concert
music takes on a disparate note
makes its mock triumphant

*

God is in the living room
his face comes through
the study in fluorescent tones

*

we were frolicking
near the carpeted silks
of red, green and blue,
spinning Arachne's web
little children in
the crisp azure of a dance.

Plath's Boy

Ted takes him to
cricket lessons

where they compare
animals in a sonnet

three poets in a family
sipping coffee

with cigarettes
in a Cezanne ashtray

walking over ghosts
on a noon stroll

dry metaphors
dancing under them

dryads spinning—
lost in the trinity.

British Isle

a gray-haired Scottish lady
& one from Montreal
speak the Queen's English
while Ireland explodes

her royal highness is
85 and Dublin is blazing
Yeats is gone and
cats are purring

matrons wear gloves at
umbrella factories
with dead poets
& Muriel Spark

fine china dust
could have lasted
but she left them
with James Joyce
and his maid.

Grandma and the Football Team

Grandma didn't always
hang with the football team,
sometimes she played hockey or
ice-skated with Chinese waiters.

Ida—pale, thin and hunch-backed at 80—
was no Leon Trotsky,
nor was she Michelangelo's David.

Ida lived with Julia Grossman,
a lady who wore makeup over her skin cancer.
Ida worried if Julia stole her cottage cheese.

One weekend, while her children went to England,
her children's children, that is,
the burnout Jimmy Hendrix fans
who did acid and smoked pot,
drank a few beers and made fun of the queers,
the incarnates of New Jersey,
sophisticated and aesthetic culture,
decided to have a party.

But they did not invite Grandma,
they locked her in the bedroom,
with Ida in her nighties,
while the boys in the band
and the girls in the boys
went rollicking through the
kitchen where Ida, twenty minutes before,
ate gefilte fish.

She took off her stockings,
letting the long toes rip,
when in came Lakewood, New Jersey's finest,

like a herd of erect penises,
to celebrate with a woman whose heart valves
were rustier than old bicycles.

Bras snapped
the dog Shrimpy got high
goyisha weight lifters
made love to Brooklyn Zionists.

The skinny matriarch
with a full head of gray hair
and bumps on her head
in her flowered nightgown,
where you could see her
flabby breasts bouncing,
yelled, "Eleanor! What's going on?
Eleanor—I have a heart condition!"

"We're having a party Grandma,
would you like to join?"

"Vey's mir!" she whined, screaming in Yiddish
to the Polish, Irish, and German quarterbacks.
Smoking a joint, one went up to Ida,
"Would you like a hit?"

Ida's grandson, in a veil of pot,
led her to bed,
where she snuggled under a
pink comforter
while the pot shone through
like a vapor against the window.

Seesaw

the doctor's
face came
down
purple-blue

her daddy, also a doctor,
not purple-blue,
drove to Lakewood
to get his daughter,
the future gynecologist
from the seesaw
where her brilliance
had its face smashed

moments
before a kiss
was
all
the other girl meant.

Hebrew Lamb

I broke his fifth metatarsal,
which Michelangelo and Renaissance artists,
Allen Ginsberg and Robert Mapplethorpe,
spilled urine upon.

a Jersey girl who didn't know Springsteen
or Whitman, desecrated the Greek statue
near my friend Randi's concrete garden,
where his blond locks fell
in the sweat of a flirtatious dance.

he whined, a yell so loud the Hasidim,
saying the morning *shema*, made a blessing;
the Lord should not be disturbed by
this supernal being.

he, the Olympic athlete,
a member of the Czarist gene pool,
chased after PLO terrorists
who idolized Yasser Arafat—
the man who killed children
riding to school on Egged buses.

the Garden State pimple girl,
failed math class integer equations,
lacked finesse of a soprano in Cantor's
bat mitzvah class, traipsed like an ape
through matzoh ball soup,
flying through his kibbutz kitchen
ceiling during suppertime.

he howled next to Randi who
smiled at this DNA dreamboat while
I stomped on the perfect toe that

Charles Darwin displayed in formaldehyde
for Japanese and Viennese tourists at
the Mütter Museum in Philadelphia.

Meningitis

The blonde girl
with the French braid
whose father teaches Latin
gave me a great thrill
when she said hello
on my birthday
had meningitis

I devoted an hour
to its meaning:
mosquitoes might kill her
brain, said *Dorland's*

The insects made her lie
in the hospital
while I sat in the library,
where we saw one another between pages
near pale-green bathrooms
where feminists wrote graffiti

I knew at any moment,
in those big vinyl chairs,
with ice clicking in my Coke,
she'd stare at me

*

across from the golf course,
as rain poured along the highway
and cars went to the amusement park,
past the blue-shingled house,
I decided to write her biography.

*

I phoned to read the introduction,
but she hung up.

Waitress at the Red Moon Pizzeria

When I first met you, you were a waitress at the Red Moon Pizzeria
and Albert Schwartz said you made pizza boxes for $1.50 an hour
and sued the owner while cockroaches and mice scuttled on the
floor, and Maggie Jones bragged you were in her bed watching *Pink
Flamingos.*

 I wanted to kiss your cheek, feel your fury for a minute, but couldn't
drive my bike near your German Shepherd on Sycamore Avenue.

And when you and Hank got married I wrote asking how you were,
if you read my poetry and newsletters, but he didn't answer, and then
I came across a short-haired photo of you on Facebook near a train;
was like, "oh my God!"/a word/phrase/you always use; a nymph
swimmer/lustrous eyes/a soul not marred by God's sonorous arias.

In a strike on Bach's piano, in the midst of St. Augustine's concerto,
you sent me a message—*the thunderbolt font dancing in elliptical
illusions until hours/days/a week passed* and you didn't answer so
Mother said "forget her."

While she lay in the New Brunswick ER, I e-mailed to see if your
ears were open, if the symphonies you possessed could mix with the
intermittent melodies of my heart.

I dreamt your mom hired me but didn't take the job because she was
you in a black suit as I flew in your house and you'd be on the bed
and disappear.

Then Susan, the former track star/now savant paraplegic, said you're
in "the program" with boys who drowned me, and maybe you'd get
her sober.

Alicia, whom we knew but didn't know we knew, called to meet in Philly but I didn't know her or that you knew her and declined to meet her.

I was angry and deleted you until you appeared as a boy in a plastic bubble redefining his words as he says them. It took months/weeks after my mom died for you to write.

Thought you were nuts/speaking forever on the phone/the jittering sensation of your mind on the moon/the matters that lilted in your brain on cocaine but were now quite sober, thank you Jesus and members of AA.

Wanted off the fucking phone, but you kept talking talking talking. Other women I could date didn't divulge heroin addictions in thirty seconds; could walk in profoundly safe conversations along country roads; why not date normal fifty-year-olds with inferior orthodontic work, not adolescent icons who put single bullets through my chest?

You with clacking teeth, unmetered laughter, the way you sometimes cry or breathe in our bed or listen to me snore for ten minutes.

This Brooklyn/Perth Amboy/North Carolina chick who wouldn't call, but I saw you in my mom's sheets, nestled in their dust, you, the sweet girl, waiting for me to touch you, feel your lips and breasts, smell your skin against mine and stomach like a light bulb underneath so tightly wound that laughs when I tell crippled men "to fuck off."

You made me an hour late for Chanukah and I was like, *I've had enough of this shit*, met *Kinder* and Daddy who spoke like an authentic Jew-WASP with a Pulitzer Prize-winning cancer book on his coffee table, and you said "wash your hands in the bathroom."

No one has ever told me to wash my hands.

And your dad was mad cause I "made him and his grandchildren eat late," though I'm a brilliant conversationalist and have read the entire library of Belleville, New Jersey.
And your momma, shrunk since fifth grade, served us spinach.

My green texts were longer than your grays
You felt smothered like a senior citizen in a hand-knitted Terracotta
afghan

After you met my cousin, whom you liked/hated/wanted her boots and Gene and his gay friends and his aneurysm pal in a crowded restaurant, I made you feel like a six-year-old going for the cab and demanded you "give the cabbie your credit card!" Shouted: "We're LESBIANS! We like poontang!"

Thought you'd jump off the Walt Whitman Bridge or throw me.
I left you stranded in the bus station, you and van Gogh bonding, which got me jealous, like when I envisioned you were having an affair with the aneurysm lady.

So here we are in a pause again, and I'm the pizzeria waitress with a crush on you, making boxes.

Absentis

Can't bribe myself to shut down
in an elevator and suffocate
drown in worms along the river
listening to classical music
you run in my soul
hide in corners
squirt stems of flowers
ballet in Lincoln Center
genteel feet along reality
make God strut
you used to walk
with Agnes and Mrs. Kinsey where
bushes lie and highways hum.

Premonition

Tingle
she makes me tingle
slurring my words
she slurs her words
not like Truman Capote
snake in the grass
amid the coffee conversation in high-rise apartments
where children have frappuccinos
I see her lips
tiny flesh bulbs
weave my brain
I grapple with God
in a few minutes we
are diving

Baptism

over sushi and ice cream
you said it might kill me
I'm like *naaah*, I'm not
bulimic, and you're like *yeah, you're gonna die*,
call me, if you need to stop,
send melodies over the guitar
while you sit in the church
parking lot after a meeting
or maybe one of your friends,
with coke melting,
can feed me.

Confusion at the Heavenly Mass

I wanted to send her Zen
flowers anonymously because
her beauty never ceased
Everyone knows
a night in bed with her
is God next to you
Yet I blew it under the covers
There one day
gone tomorrow
Dante didn't have Beatrice
but I had Julie
between my lips
till love passed like a new Dionysian language
that twisted between my pulse
Lip-synced new phrases she no longer loved
and the fish went swimming with other salmon.

*

All the sanctimonious singers dance at her feet
Spellbound St. Thomas Aquinas himself wordless
a fountain spun
Godliness
like Mr. Graham Greene and his sainthood
on endless bouquet trips
taking tipsy-eyed learning sessions to the moon
back and forth
interpretive dance sessions
baptismal recovery where God at his peak
doesn't even understand the room
she has left him in.

Eel

slipping on
the bank
the long-lost bird
who flew down from the
apple tree
Darwin's missing link
who kissed three Neanderthals
in their King-sized bed

The Goodbye Song

Yesterday I was John Hinckley, Jr.
messaging you and your sister
envisioning there'd be lawsuits
Maybe they'd put me in a mental institution
for violating the laws of nature
by sending you a Keith Haring puzzle
You'd love the watercolor splash of blue boys dancing against
the black/white skinny men.
But no alphabets came
I tapped the receiver hoping for green
Don't mean cops, money or humor.

My self-esteem keeps me bottled,

though I'd like to send you a silk scarf,

with ivy-covered fields.

Grandma in the Trailer Park

Grandma grew up
in a Newark high-rise
where people borrowed
cottage cheese and eggs

at 82 she was
kicked out of an apartment
because Orthodox Jews were
building a *shul*
and a kosher butcher shop
no room for her soap
operas and hamburgers
frying in water

in Jackson, NJ, we
put Grandma in a trailer
the size of a studio
with a lady named Trinity
who believed in Jesus but didn't
preach to Grandma, who
couldn't walk well and had
difficulty getting to religious services

Grandma ate gefilte fish along the Formica
counter where Mickey Rourke
spilled beer in *The Wrestler*

the steps weren't high
the bed was near the bathroom
by the kitchen
with toast burning
and *Jeopardy!* playing on TV

Fostoria, Ohio

a large slab of concrete
is the train station
a cat walks by
my brother said that
felines in Ohio are
fierce bobcats that kill
at 1 a.m. in the morning
serial murderers do not
approach the Amtrak platform
they stay in the bushes
while a white Yugo
and a balding brother
who complains about rednecks
that gave him the wrong directions
approaches the platform
we sit in his car
eating doughnuts and
go home to Columbus, Ohio
where I sleep all
week watching *Days of Our Lives*
Roman Brady
climbs the pyramids
Ohio gets culture through the
television set
we see the best of
MASH and the
worst of Ed Sullivan
the entire week is a reunion
with ourselves
and our brother
who drove us to Fostoria
he leaves us home to read Henry Miller
and watch Bo Brady
sleep with women I find attractive

I get up at 2 p.m.
with caffeine stains and
James Wright hangovers
while my brother
hits on women in bars
I go to 12-step meetings
that are like David Duke rallies
and ask him to drive me back to Fostoria
his Yugo breaks down and
he rents a car and talks
with waitresses who chauffeur
football teams to Fostoria
they win the state championship
and give us coffee and
directions as
he threatens to
abort me for not
having faith in his ability
not to ride into the Twilight Zone
on the cold Ohio highway
we stop near beer-drinking
men who tell us
how to get the New York train
in the remaining three minutes
but I remember the time he got
us lost in Montreal for three hours
we go center in the dark of a Stephen King deli
he drops me off
I eat sandwiches
he made until
I arrive in New York, New York
without handouts
and rummage my life
which could have been as remote
as a concrete platform

Me and Larry King and His Wife

Mrs. King is angrier than
the Earth's smallest man,
for I, her Jewish maid,
use Ajax, not Mrs. Meyer's.
She prefers free-trade rags,
Mexican housekeepers in pink
aprons who diligently assent to
cleaning toilets.

*

I am demoted to "baby-sitter,"
have sex in their basement,
peak through bottom windows,
where ground meets weeds,
my boyfriend letting me suck
his big lollipop in the midst of
Larry's Ethan Allen furniture.

The Kings know not the
sanctimonious acts
committed against them
and their expensive refrigerator
where ham and Worcestershire sauce meet
lipstick and herring.

Mrs. King puts me on probation,
Her boys yell: *you need Zoloft!*
I whine in their reality show,
protest to Larry's lapin ears;
he is busy with Michael Jackson's
ghost and celebrities from the screen.

Sandstorm

On a living room couch, she tells me
her new girlfriend is Saudi Arabian.
I can't compete with this Vestal
whose family discusses prurience
with the *mutaween*[8]; is frightened when gas station
attendants see her kiss. Saudi Arabia and Julie,
the women behind Hijabs, drive their car at
low volume on the Jersey Turnpike. Grandpa says,
"Saudi Arabians can also have their men/men";
my living room couch sinks.

---

[8] Islamic religious police.

Poe's Short Story

the town laughed at you
while their LPs spun in a white
apartment in Carson McCuller's novel

*

mutes with shrill teeth plucking raw fruit

*

a police lady in sweaty nylons said,
"the Negro doctor wants you to turn off
Mozart till your Grandma gets home."

*

saw you again for the first time,
a white face in a room with
other white faces

*

I skim to see if you are looking;
you offer everyone else peanuts.

*

*Momma died
then Virginia
then you*

we can't laugh about lunch boxes, stare at family members, or hold hands in the parking lot; let's say adieu, though you're alive, like in Poe's short story, when they bury you.

Before you were a chromosome I...

Played doctor with Mina as our house burned
Answered *"Red Moon Pizzeria!"* when a senator rang
Was picked up by cops for lifting my shirt
Cried when my brothers called me "2 by 4"
Set up a gynecologist's office in fifth grade
Loved Mom forty years before her death
Threw a puppy down the stairs
Stayed mute when Sari pushed me down the stairs
Smelled like body odor without knowing how to shower
Watched Zionists drag my mattress into the woods
Enraged Palestinians with an "I love Zionism" button
Got banished from the neighbor's backyard for shouting "fuck you"
Stuck my middle finger at Mr. G who called the police
Dropped Arthur Treacher's thermometer into the fryer
Got detention arguing, "Fidel Castro is a great man!"
Broke your mother's toilet seat; called her a "Stepford wife"
Swallowed a spoonful of instant coffee
Snorted cocaine during a Thomas Aquinas seminar in Princeton
Dressed as the Hulk in Jerusalem and scared Armenian sanitation
workers
Lost my virginity to an Israeli without getting herpes
Stood alone in the morning while other kids did not
Watched mean black girls steal purses from mean white girls
Drank too much with unsuspecting Brooklyn chicks
Got raped by a second-string Stanford University tennis player
Came to believe in Jesus, Mohammed, and Hare Krishna, anyone
who'd be my friend, even foreshadowed you—the gummy-bear
messiah—and this made me grin.

Jewish Girls

She lies
You believe her
She lies
You believe her
You from the same private school
Once we were all in the same ghetto
Smelly Jews with similar beards
Eating gefilte fish/underarm hairs/getting rocks thrown at us/pickles
where the Chinese have their cockroaches/fish smelling like
newspapers dipped in shit/kicked by the vociferous Poles/getting
eggs showered on us/till they electrocuted us in the fence
Then we became gold teeth in the museum
Now you take your kids to see us on Sundays
Black security guards make sure the anti-Semites don't bomb
After that you have brunch.

Chess

in moments with her kids or in-laws
who don't know we dated or kissed
lapsed into laughter from 9 to 10

I tell her son, "we have a job for you,"
like Kafka's great hunger artist
or elephants munching in Great Adventure's
safari, where we worked and didn't know

when her sister reluctantly hugs my brother
at their 20th reunion, I ask him to relive it,
he says it was gruesome, not my fault—
they hated each other in high school

I wonder if she has changed the photograph
since we spoke six months ago, if she
acknowledges my Georgia O'Keeffe postcard
with an image of D. H. Lawrence's rocking horse

I write about her Jew-hating toupee toll-booth clerk
daddy who sneaks his daughters into church
when the Hebe wife goes shopping

there are no bishops, queens or kings on board,
no black and white decimal points journeying my brain to hers,
only the eclipse of the possibility she might hate me

Death March in Austria
1938

an old woman
in yellowed wrinkles
like the patch on her arm
walks festively through bright green Austria
along lines of grass
near leather boots that kick ancient symbols

her shawl is ripped brown and white
it hung by the River's window
a good view of the Rhine

she wraps it around shoulders
bones coming in like fish

the earth's floor is my grandma's skin
sweet soap from a bath

gray-haired novel reader presses her lips against my face

foot stepping in a jigsaw puzzle

Zayde

Visits to him
in a Jewish nursing home
Maimonides' name
hangs above the elevator

The gray man
with a thick
yellow moustache says
"put your fingers in mine"

Old boys in yarmulkes
get their children
to do the same

They are quiet
while he asks for
chocolate milk

Yellowed ladies
speaking Yiddish
tell their daughters to brush
smooth gray hair

I went outside
and thought of the plum
pit we buried together
how it was supposed
to grow into a tree

I put my face against
his cheeks—
lines running
where a man
went door to door

with frozen blocks;
Leon Trotsky's grandnephew,
the ice-man socialist,
began smoking at ten
and hasn't stopped

Beneath a large gray slab
smooth as a piece
of cold rock,
I put my face

He kisses me
without teeth
the smell of tobacco in
his bristles

Tall men with skinny necks
sit next to their kids and
play cards

I adjust
his ash tray;
he sends me to get
Du Maurier cigarettes
from the vending machine

The ice man
who brought sheets
sits while the wind
blows through the corridor

I wave; he grins,
knowing our last words
might be these.

John Forbes Nash, Jr. [9]

He didn't like Jews
who studied and taught
with him, and was also not
fond of mathematicians,
but among the obscure group
dotting the universe with logic
across the blackboard—devising
game theories in a cosmos
along Santa Monica beaches
while cruising Greek-looking
boys and a girl physics major
and eventually descended into
schizophrenia in a community of
iron-pressed rugby shirts
where the firestorm in his
mind released Communist spies
in capes masquerading as integers
through loops and negatives of
neurons in the thunder which
transgressed humanity in vulgar
speeches crisscrossing with
pills until God threw an
ordinal and he returned a kiss.

---

[9] John Forbes Nash, Jr. (1928-2015) was an American mathematician whose works in game theory, differential geometry, and partial differential equations have provided insight into the factors that govern chance and events inside complex systems in daily life; he suffered from schizophrenia.

.

Tiger Lilies

My father follows
as the tiger lilies
bloom
they are lions
with petals
for ears
and their long tails
come
from the earth
my daddy stops the
car to smell them
he plucks one from someone's
garden and puts
it to his nose
my father has loved
a few things
his wife
Darryl Strawberry
and the family
of orange friends
that tick each
July when the summer
enters the sun and
the rain drips upon
the car
where you still
see his orange friends
gliding in the wind.

CD Poem

His name was Joe
I met him selling $2 CDs
and asked if he liked doing
that at his age
Joe said that he once
sold 17 trailers of lambs
so he's really done everything,
in addition to his CDs
"17 trailers of lambs,"
I asked, "were they alive?"
I saw meat being
dispensed: little lamb heads
in a Pathmark butcher's bin
tongues being plucked
from the soul of their kin
"Lamps!" he said, "lamps!"

Princeton

I was intimidated by its
gothic structures in contrast
to the strip malls of Jersey
but now I'm on Nassau Street
drinking stale coffee and
chewing my nails while
reading Fitzgerald's *Ulysses*
maybe the people are a little
stuffy and not as scruffy as
the homeless in my neighborhood
which doesn't make it better
or Princeton worse but makes
me wonder where the intimidation
and illusions have collapsed all
these years of layered thoughts
giving this small street redemption
with residents also anxious to
get the train to New York.

Sister

She is like a sonic boom.
She purchases pie but licks it first.
She hears the camels of Holland while smelling the odors
of London.
Her mind is warped by the perfume of sewage that drips through her
auditory canals.
Lydia flies to London on a Banana Republic airplane.
Lydia walks to the Banana Republic on a London airplane.
She circulates among Hindus who are praying and asks if she can
have a metaphysical discussion with them.
"Poontang" is not a word my sister would use.
If my sister were to use "poontang," her friends would stop taking
her to backgammon.
Place that mambo rhythm up your buttock sister fucker dude.
The blue MOMA is under construction; my sister says taking the
train to Queens to see art is a contradictory statement.
The moon has holes that pinch it, my sister noted when I asked her
why we don't travel there.
Lydia went skinny dipping in Alaska during the summertime.
I don't like when the random voices in my head ignore me.
Sister will go skinny dipping if she travels to Alaska in the
summertime.
Feathered frogs.
Hammers will untie me!
Trés bien!
*"Stop bombing Afghanistan—you're not any more moral than the
Taliban!" yelled the removed hands from the maimed thieves who
had been reprimanded during the Taliban era; they were screaming
at the American soldiers.*
The odor of London drips like perfume rotting.
Lydia inhales pathos as some might reindeers on a highway.

95

Prayer

Blessed art thou
Oh Lord our God
For thine is the kingdom
The power
Glory Glory Glory
Hallelujah
My teacher hit me with
a ruler
But that was long
before my parents
showed me films
about the Holocaust when
I was ten
Catholics had rosary beads
I had Auschwitz
There has been more
God in my lungs
than cigarette smoke
although my grandfather
smoked when he was
10 but lived until 94
and they tell me my
fat content may help
a poor artist eat
Can I dump the
fat somewhere?
God will you help me
lose weight?
This is what happens
when I go on a diet:
I ask for his forgiveness.
Blessed art thou
Oh Lord our God
Keeper of the faith. Amen.

Orgasm on Yom Kippur

humming through
the water faucet
I take breaths of
Lauren Hutton

legs find
radiation
from the metallic
idol
who thrusts me
to celestial
spheres of water sports

near shower
curtains
my mother
hovers above this
sacrilege
in
polyester
vestments

"pharmaceutical majors,
PhD scholars, and
lawyers," she declares,
"will get increasingly
sharp pains
in their vertebrae
if they illicitly
find pleasure in
the bathtub"

I break a disc
like a pebble falling
in the midst of
God's sacred words

Ezra Pound and Poontang

When I was 27
I got drunk in women's bars
Brought ladies home
Read them Ezra Pound
Their makeup smeared
with Jack Daniel's stanzas

I didn't have Grandma to hug
but a slightly demonic
lover who didn't know
me except I was schooled
in anti-Semitic modernists
who did radio shows for Mussolini

When I was 27
I didn't understand why chicks
without dicks came crawling
into my bed and listened to
defiant cantos on usury
though I am a Jew

Mr. Pound and I
womanizing as rockets flew
in the Middle East
cuddled till 3 p.m.
Women who drank the Earth
while Ezra slept in our soul.

Fidel Castro at the Rambles[10]

"I don't want to be reborn as a factory-farm chicken," he said as he
fucked four Colombian circus midgets.
Before they became his concubines, the Crips pillaged them.
Transgender nuns squished the boys between subway cars.
Siamese cats chased these venerable mice who
screamed for their Harlem Prince, who was white;
a Volvo filled with cream puffs;
a megaphone inhaling the Earth's diamonds.
George W. Bush could not have prevented this tight rope walker
from disseminating the radicalism of Islam in their crevices.
A bomb could not be stopped.
Numerous chickens in Maryland factories would be slaughtered
while dwarfs danced on his wooden floors.
They feasted on avocado, sushi, and tofu chili with mixed greens.
A pancake or two slipped down the esophagus.
Mrs. Henry, on the second floor, was alarmed when her pipes rattled.
But like Fidel, he tired.
He threw them back to subway rats, where police officers gave
manikins a citation, which they couldn't pay.
They were incarcerated in Riker's Island, where tomcats prowled
loudly in a nearby cell.
The Harlem Prince went on to Edward, a monk from the Tibetan
Fields of China, whom he found pressed against a latrine.

---

[10] "The Rambles" is an area in Central Park, New York City, where gay men meet
for anonymous sex.

Lady in Suburbia

she lived in her brain:
green mazes,
dallying consonants,
metaphors dangling on her spine;
tingling sensations on
a windshield wiper

birds sang AM music,
elevator sonatas,
Wagnerian notes
that were middle class
flies falling
on your desk

she drove through
ravines in her head
filled with vines
while rain played against
Paul McCartney

Jennifer's Stately Nipples

Through the brown silk of Fairfield County
furry little beasts
lie underneath the sheath

They trickle with rain
in the shower stall
against her rock and roll football player

Upon the bed
Jennifer's stately nipples
dance on his hairy chest
Queen Elizabeth against Mike Tyson

In soliloquies of mammaries and sweat
they keep abreast of world affairs
steam rising like the smoke of oil refineries

For Jennifer's stately nipples
stand firm with desire
harder than William Kennedy Smith
they pounce against the Bob Dylan quarterback
and he submits to their arrogance

Why I Can't Marry a WASP from Connecticut:
A Revelation Received While Waiting at 125th Street

I fell in love on 125th Street
watching the snow come down

her lips opened and closed like a clam
her Chapstick was moist like unwashed underpants
her emotions were strawberries being crushed in a blender
she could suspend fear in a movie theater
and watch Anthony Hopkins steal people's tongues

I wanted to be featured
in a wedding announcement with her:

"Eleanor Foster Leech
daughter of Harold Jones Foster Leech
was married to Andrea Jones Chaucer
Daughter of Ant Farm Recipient
Chaucer Foster Jones"

She was reading a book about Namibian psychotics
by her father who taught histrionics at Yale

I was skimming *The New York Post*:
"Bob Dylan dyes his underarm hair blue and white
to support leftist Zionists"

While drug addicts sold tokens on 125th Street,
I felt like a leech of good lineage—
a New Jersey-blooded bacterial organism
who watched *All in the Family*
and attended EST seminars in Piscataway
and smoked at truck stations
where Allen Ginsberg used to urinate

for I had graduated Ocean County College
and could never marry a WASP from Connecticut
or an inebriated socialist from Westchester
or perform bestiality on Maine-bred lobsters
or live off American Home Foods stocks
while reading Wallace Stevens
or date Jewish dermatologists
with epidermal layers of Ivy League inferiority

History is a Nightmare

"History is a nightmare from which I am trying to awake," James Joyce, *Ulysses*

Maybe the mail
in England is too slow
or Kevin Smith
won't invite me to his crucifixion
or my Hasidic friend Q
was killed by Palestinians
on her way to chin plucking
in a religious settlement
or Mother threatens
to cut my tongue if
I tell my brother
that his birthmark came
from a Tupperware container she
swallowed while pregnant
and Aunt Wanda
has hairy arm pits, which
has been noted by Rastafarian
scientists working
on a cure for baldness
or an El Salvadoran boss
laughs like a train having orgasm
in the middle of a Guatemalan insurgency
bombing children and trucks
while Auschwitz nuns
drink tea in morbid indifference
above the grave site of
Zyklon B shower stalls
These are reasons
why *History is a nightmare*
or that Herman Hesse's writing
got bad when he used
Eastern philosophy
I much preferred his Nietzsche

before the Holocaust
or I have a crush on Nazis
in uniform who live in Russia
and are part Jewish
These are all reasons: my
dog Henry has black marks on
his testicles—he's going to
perish and no more
golden retriever chewing underpants
or perhaps Clinton is a Jehovah's Witness
who converts go-go dancers
and Newt Gingrich's name is Elroy
and he's a competing Arkansas dairy
farmer who never recovered from
the peanut farmer who fucked him over
and O. J. didn't murder but hired
Colin Ferguson as defense attorney
So perhaps history was the nightmare
and coffee lurks in me like a luminous
cavity because I have no health insurance
or my Uncle Harold breeds
hundreds of felines in Toledo
kittens purring for his milk kiss
or the times I put Pepsi up my
nose and thought it was Coke
or peed in nursery school and
stayed afterwards to clean it up
so maybe Stephen Dedalus was right
when he urinated on himself
about history and Bloom and Molly's
long chapter sentences, and maybe
history is herstory from which the
hisses are waking up.
1995.

Shorn

Smirks bypass me on the highway
lingering thoughts that were her fingers
sleeping in bed with taciturn felines
I enclose my arms in hers
Feel a murmur between us
The hesitant gestures contain me.
I pray, but her aunt, my God, and our mother don't listen.
I talk blankly in the parking lot, remembering
the night we spent on my mom's bed,
among the dead sheets, where the body lay, a few weeks before.
I graze lightly. Sweetly. Without remorse.
The reticent, no delicate, way, she pronounces *Rs*
Forces sound to inhabit space
I can listen for hours, my shoulder on her lips.
Mere illusions sustain me.

§

About the Author

Photo by Pedro Silva

Eleanor Levine interviewed Abbie Hoffman when he came out of hiding; John Kennedy, Jr., at Brown University; Liz Smith, John Ashbery, Quentin Crisp, Noam Chomsky, Matt Dillon and others, in her literary zine, *The Eleanor Levine Newsletter*. For twenty years she lived with Henry Miller and Virginia Woolf, her dogs, in New York City, before moving to Roanoke, VA, where she received an MFA in Creative Writing from Hollins University.

Her work has appeared in *Fiction, The Evergreen Review, The Denver Quarterly, Midway Journal, The Toronto Quarterly, Pank, Hobart, Fiction Southeast, The Kentucky Review, Dos Passos Review, Barely South Review, Connotations Press, Monkeybicycle, Everyday Genius, Artichoke Haircut, BlazeVOX, Milk Magazine, Northwind Magazine, The California State Quarterly, Prime Mincer, Happy, Penumbra, The Coachella Review, OVS Magazine, Gertrude, Atticus Review, Fanzine, fortyouncebachelors.com, Thrice Fiction, Barrelhouse, Lunch Ticket Magazine, The Red Booth Review, Wilde, Educe Journal, Milk and Honey: A Celebration of Jewish Lesbian Poetry* (nominated for a 2012 Lambda Literary Award), *Downtown Poets* (anthology), *New York Sex* (anthology), *The Wall Street Journal, The Washington Blade, The New York Blade, The New York Amsterdam News, Litro Magazine (UK), Storm Cellar, Artemis Journal, Literateur (UK), Roadside Fiction (Ireland), S/tick (Canada), Intima: A Journal of Narrative Medicine, IthacaLit, Foliate Oak Literary Magazine, Right Hand Pointing, Juked, Gone Lawn, The Stockholm Review of Literature, Menacing Hedge* and *Crack the Spine* . She has work forthcoming in the *Tulane Review* and *The MacGuffin*. Eleanor is currently a copy editor and lives in Philadelphia, Pennsylvania, with her dog Morgan.

About the Photographer

Brian Healey is an artist and lawyer whose street photography, sculpture and multimedia pieces have been included in numerous shows at galleries in Brooklyn and New York City, including the Leslie-Lohman Museum of Gay and Lesbian Art. Brian currently lives in New York City, where he scrutinizes his life through a lens.

Previous Appearances

"Why I Can't Marry a WASP from Connecticut: A Revelation Received While Waiting at 125th Street," *Artemis Journal*, April 2015.

"Concertos in the Living Room" and "Grandma in the Trailer Park," *Kentucky Review* online edition, http://kentuckyreview.org/index.php/issues2/2015/poetry-2015/item/376-elevinebio, and their annual print edition (January 2016).

"Barnegat," *Ithaca Lit*, http://ithacalit.com/eleanor-levine.html, Fall 2014.

"John Forbes Nash, Jr," *Intima: A Journal of Narrative Medicine*, Fall 2014.

"Zayde," *The Dos Passos Review*, http://thedospassosreview.com/zayde/, June 2014.

"Waitress at the Red Moon Pizzeria," in *The Literateur Magazine* (UK), http://literateur.com/waitress-at-the-red-moon-pizzeria/, June 2014.

"Plath's Boy," *Artemis Journal*, May 2014.

"Fostoria, Ohio," *Hot Street*, Winter 2013-2014 issue.

"ενέργεια," *Barrelhouse*, Politics issue, http://www.barrelhousemag.com/#!%CE%B5%CE%BD%CE%AD%CF%81%CE%B3%CE%B5%CE%B9%CE%B1-by-Eleanor-Levine/cge1/8B61A190-F483-4215-B641-88CC5F4B53B2, November 16, 2013.

"High School," *Everyday Genius*, http://www.everyday-genius.com/2013/11/eleanor-levine.html, November 13, 2013.

"poem about prunes," *Wilde Magazine*, Spring 2013.

"Before you were a chromosome I…," *the NewerYork*, http://theneweryork.com/chromosome-list-of-accomplishments-by-eleanor-levine/, May 2013.

"History is a Nightmare," *Artichoke Haircut*, Volume Five, Spring 2013 (April 2013).

"Train," "Ida," and "E's Baseball," *Fanzine*, http://thefanzine.com/author/eleanorl/, January 16, 2013.

"Daddy," *Northwind Magazine*, http://www.northwindmagazine.com/print/5/daddy.html?autoprint=true, Winter 2013.

"First Girlfriend," *Bicycle Review*, Women's Issue, http://www.thebicyclereview.net/19.html, December 15, 2012.

"The Goodbye Song," "Artificial Limbs" (http://educejournal.com/2012/12/06/fall-2012-issue-no-3-poetry-by-eleanor-levine-digital-issue-only-5/) and "Confusion at the Heavenly Mass," *Educe*, Issue 3, Fall 2012.

"Thysanura," "Minnie," "The Follower" and "At Delicious Orchards," *Blaze VOX12*, http://www.blazevox.org/BX%20Covers/BXFall2012/Eleanor%20Levine%20-%20Fall%202012.pdf, Fall 2012.

"Me and Larry King and His Wife," *Red Booth Review*, http://redboothreview.blogspot.com/2012/07/me-and-larry-king-and-his-wife-eleanor.html, Vol 8: 1, 2012.

"Grandma and the Football Team," *Lunch Ticket* (Antioch University of Los Angeles), http://lunchticket.org/grandma-and-the-football-team/, Spring 2012.

"Hebrew Lamb" originally appeared as "The Aryan of Jews," in *Forty Ounce Bachelors*, Volume 1, Issue 10, March 1, 2012.

"The Electric Menorah," *OVS Magazine*, Spring 2012 Issue.

"Orgasm on Yom Kippur," *Milk and Honey: A Celebration of Jewish Lesbian Poetry* (A Midsummer's Night Press), 2011 (anthology).

"Mammaliga," "Pallidotomy," *Artichoke Haircut*, Volume 2, July 11, 2011.

"Two Friends," *The Toronto Quarterly*, Issue 6, 2010.

"Lunch Drawing" originally appeared as "A Greek Penumbra Spills Itself" in *Taj Mahal Review*, Vol. 3, Number 1, June 2004.

"Sister" originally appeared as "My Sister," "Prayers," *The Bayou Review* (University of Houston-Downtown Literary and Visual Arts Journal) Fall 2004.

"Princeton," originally appeared as "The Princeton Poem," in *California Quarterly* (California State Poetry Society), Vol. 28, No. 3, 2002.

"Tiger Lilies" originally appeared as "My Father and the Tiger Lilies"; and "CD Poem" in *Downtown Poets* (anthology)—(Montclair Takilma Books), 1999, authors featured: Colette Inez, Sapphire, Tom Savage and others.

"My Dead Roommate," *Onion River Review* (Goddard College), Vol. 2, No. 1, Fall, 1994.

Made in the USA
Middletown, DE
24 October 2020

21699998R00066